We Need
WORMS

AMY HAYES

PowerKiDS
press.

New York

Published in 2016 by The Rosen Publishing Group, Inc.
29 East 21st Street, New York, NY 10010

First Edition

Editor: Caitie McAneney
Book Design: Mickey Harmon

Photo Credits: Cover (image) wawritto/Shutterstock.com; cover, pp. 1, 3–4, 6, 8–9, 11–12, 16–18, 21, 22–24 (background) Click Bestsellers/Shutterstock.com; p. 5 Kokhanchikov/Shutterstock.com; p. 7 Maryna Pleshkun/Shutterstock.com; pp. 8, 22 PHOTO FUN/Shutterstock.com; p. 10 clearviewstock/Shutterstock.com; p. 13 Stephen Dalton/Minden Pictures/Getty Images; p. 14 (inset) CHAINFOTO24/ Shutterstock.com; p. 14–15 (main), 19 schankz/Shutterstock.com; p. 16 spiro/ Shutterstock.com; p. 17 (centipede) underworld/Shutterstock.com; p.17 (ants) Hurst Photo/Shutterstock.com; p. 17 (spider) Plamuekwhan/Shutterstock.com; p. 20 Fotokostic/Shutterstock.com.

Library of Congress Cataloging-in-Publication Data

Hayes, Amy, author.
We need worms / Amy Hayes.
    pages cm. — (Creatures we can't live without)
Includes bibliographical references and index.
ISBN 978-1-4994-0986-4 (pbk.)
ISBN 978-1-4994-1027-3 (6 pack)
ISBN 978-1-4994-1049-5 (library binding)
1. Earthworms—Juvenile literature. 2. Soil formation—Juvenile literature. I. Title. II.
Series: Creatures we can't live without.
QL391.A6H39 2016
592.64—dc23
                                        2015014823

Manufactured in the United States of America

CONTENTS

WE NEED WORMS!

Have you ever seen worms squirming around on the sidewalk after a rainstorm? Maybe you've seen worms in a garden, moving through the dirt. With no arms and no legs, you might not think these little creatures have a big **impact** on the world around them. However, worms are an important part of their **ecosystem**.

Everything in nature, from the grass that grows to the birds singing up in the trees, depends on worms. We need worms for flowers, crops, and trees to grow. Let's dig in to learn more about worms!

People say earthworms are a sign of healthy soil. That's because worms keep the soil healthy by living in it!

WHAT ARE WORMS, ANYWAY?

Worms found in the ground are called earthworms. Some people believe there are around 3,000 species, or types, of earthworms. Others believe there are more than 7,000.

Worms are invertebrates, which means they have no spine, or backbone. They're made up of segments, or parts, called annuli. The first segment holds their mouth.

Earthworms can live in soil, but also in puddles and under rocks and logs. There are three main types of earthworms—litter dwellers, topsoil dwellers, and subsoil dwellers. They're named for the soil areas where they make their home. Each of the earthworm types helps the **environment** in different ways.

CREATURE CLUE

Worms can be very long. Austrailia's giant Gippsland earthworms can grow to nearly 6.5 feet (2 m) long!

Worms have no bones at all, which is why they can curl their body like this.

WHERE ARE WORMS?

The three main types of worms are divided by where they live in the soil. Litter dwellers live on and above the ground. They live in leaves, grass, and **compost** piles. They like warm, wet areas and don't eat a lot of soil.

Topsoil dwellers live in the first two to three inches (5 to 7.6 cm) of soil. They **burrow** sideways throughout the soil. Subsoil dwellers burrow straight down into the soil, sometimes as far as five to six feet (1.5 to 1.8 m)! They keep their burrows open so they can return to the surface.

Worms that live in the first few inches of soil are topsoil dwellers.

Earthworms and Their Homes

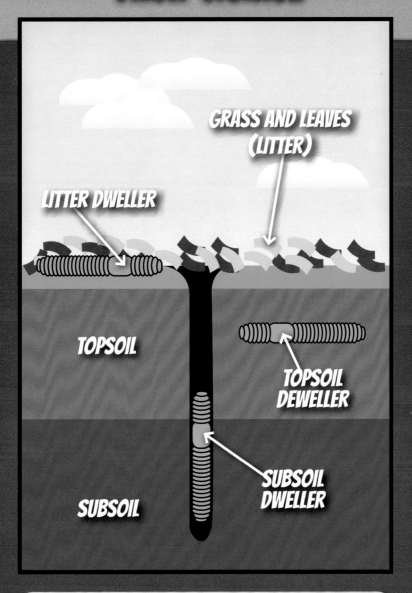

GRASS AND LEAVES (LITTER)

LITTER DWELLER

TOPSOIL

TOPSOIL DEWELLER

SUBSOIL DWELLER

SUBSOIL

Each type of worm lives in a different part of the soil.

These worms have made a lot of air pockets for water to collect in!

HARDWORKING BURROWERS

Earthworms create pockets of air as they burrow through the soil. The pockets of air help break up the soil, which makes it easier for plants to grow. The air pockets also make it easier for rain to settle in the ground.

When it rains, water falls through the soil and gathers in the small burrows. The water makes the dirt soft and wet, which is good for growing plants. The air pockets made by worms also help prevent flooding. If it rains hard, the rainwater collects throughout the soil instead of sitting on top of the ground or running off.

CREATURE CLUE

One study found that earthworms can eat up to 40 tons (36 mt) of soil per acre every year.

MIXING UP THE SOIL

When worms move through the soil, they end up eating many **microorganisms** and lots of dirt. Worms drag soil along with them as they tunnel through the ground. Subsoil dwellers move deep into the earth. They can bring up lots of new dirt that hasn't been close to the surface for years.

By mixing the soil, earthworms spread out **nutrients**. This makes the soil healthier for plants. Many people think worms help completely change the makeup of the first six inches (15 cm) of soil every 10 to 20 years. Without them, the soil wouldn't be healthy and plants couldn't grow well.

CREATURE CLUE

The famous **naturalist** Charles Darwin called worms "nature's ploughs" because they mix up the soil the way farm plows do.

This earthworm burrow shows how worms dig down in the first few inches of the ground.

CREATURE CLUE

Worm feces, or waste, are called casts.

Worms that live on the top of the soil eat many different kinds of plant matter, such as leaves. These worms are eating matter from a compost pile.

RECYCLING REMAINS

When plants and animals die, their remains are full of nutrients that are an important part of the ecosystem. **Decomposition** is a process that makes those nutrients available to living things again. Worms are an important part of decomposition!

As a worm burrows through the soil, it eats remains. As it eats, it breaks down the nutrients into smaller pieces. The worm's waste is then full of small, easily available nutrients. The nutrients in the worm's waste are then ready to be recycled by microorganisms. Worms are so important to decomposition that people buy worms to put in their compost piles to help the compost decompose.

PART OF THE FOOD WEB

Food webs are a way to show connections among plants and animals. We call them "webs" because all plants and animals in an ecosystem depend on one another.

This bird, called a thrush, enjoys eating a worm as a morning meal.

CENTIPEDES

ANTS

SPIDERS

CREATURE CLUE

Earthworm predators also include
bugs, such as ants, centipedes,
and spiders.

Worms don't just help the
ecosystem with soil or decomposition.
Worms are an important part of the
food web as prey, or animals that are
eaten by other animals. Just as worms
eat nutrients from soil, other animals
eat worms for the nutrients they need.
Birds, beetles, and even small mammals
such as moles eat worms. Some
endangered land snails in New Zealand
depend on worms as a source of food.

AN EARTHWORM'S HOME

Earthworms do well in lots of environments. However, there are certain things worms need. Most of all, worms need a damp, or somewhat wet, place to live. They lose a lot of water through their skin, so they need to live in a wet environment.

Worms go into hibernation, or a deep sleep-like state, if it gets too cold. Worms like to live in temperatures between 50 and 60 degrees Fahrenheit (10 and 15.5 degrees Celsius).

Worms also need certain types of food. They like to eat **manure**, as well as bits of leaves and other types of plants.

CREATURE CLUE

The type of soil can also be important. Worms prefer wet, soft soil to sandy or clay-like soil.

These worms are happily snacking on manure. It's full of nutrients!

HUMANS CAUSING HARM

People have made big changes to the world around them. Farms, cities, gardens, and lawns all exist because people put them there. When people make changes to their environment, it can harm other animals.

Worms are sometimes harmed by the changes people make. When farmers use the same piece of land over and over again for the same crop, it changes the soil. Some crops don't add the right nutrients to the soil and are bad for worms. They stop burrowing and helping out the soil. Certain types of **pesticides** can also hurt worms, though there are many that are safe to use.

Farmers have to be careful to make sure they don't decrease worm populations.

HOW CAN WE HELP?

Luckily, worms are pretty amazing creatures. When humans create environments where worms can live, they will **thrive**. Farmers love worms because of how good they are for soil and crops. Farmers can make nice environments for worms by switching where crops are planted regularly and trying to use pesticides that are safe for worms to be around.

Worms prevent flooding, mix soil together, break down nutrients, and are prey for other animals. Next time you see a worm crawling in the dirt, think about all the things it does to help the environment around it.

GLOSSARY

burrow: To dig or move through the ground.

compost: A pile of waste that decomposes and is used for fertilizer.

decomposition: The breakdown of plant and animal matter.

ecosystem: All the living things in an area.

endangered: In danger of dying out.

environment: Everything that surrounds a living thing.

impact: Strong effect.

manure: Matter that makes soil rich, especially the waste of farm animals.

microorganism: A living thing so small it can only be seen with a microscope.

naturalist: A person who studies nature.

nutrient: Something taken in by a plant or animal that helps it grow and stay healthy.

pesticide: Matter used to kill pests.

thrive: To grow successfully.

INDEX

WEBSITES

Due to the changing nature of Internet links, PowerKids Press has developed an online list of websites related to the subject of this book. This site is updated regularly. Please use this link to access the list: www.powerkidslinks.com/cwcl/worm